Foreword from Bernard Wrigley:

I've always written down words, made them rhyme, and then usually put a tune to them. Sometimes they end up as humorous monologues. I thought that's what Jim did, too. But he does much more. Jim is a poet, and a proper one. He writes about anything and everything, just as the mood takes him. Philosophy, reflections, anger, tenderness, life in general, and, of course, just plain daft. It's the "just plain daft" that sprinkles sunshine on otherwise serious topics - and it's the serious topics that stop it from being looked on as too light-hearted. It's a powerful brew of poetry, prose, and off the wall.

To quote one of the poems in this collection:

"But just 'cos it rhymes

Doesn't make it a poem."

If the old COI (Central Office of Information) was ever to be restarted, then Jim should be in charge to put all matters in perspective.

Don't read them too quickly.

These are writings to savour.

Thanks, Jim!

DIGITAL BLUES

Are there QI codes for uncertain

Bar codes for feeling crap

AI that gives a frail soul hope

When the bad stuff lands in your lap

Satnavs that lead you to heaven

Do iPhones prepare you for dying

A YouTube vid to reverse what you did

And an App to help you stop crying

FACTS

He wants to believe she loves him

He wants to believe it is true

So he filters out all of the evidence

That doesn't support that view

Being completely open-minded

And accepting the heart attacks

Doesn't give him that warm inner glow

So he tries to ignore the facts

Similar to most things these days

You decide what to take, what to leave

Cherry-pick from the deluge of data

To believe what you want to believe.

TATTOO

Sailors and Hells Angels

Ex-Army, builders, merry few

When I was a lad not many people

Showed off a tattoo

Now everybody's got one

On their arms, bums, chests and thighs

You have to wear next to nothin'

Or folks won't realise

That you support Man City

Your first love was called Frank

And that scene from Lord o'the Rings

Cost an overdraft from the bank

They used to indicate you were hard

Especially tattoos on your face

Now even nuns have "I love Jesus"

Inscribed in a secret place.

His first love was called Carol

Had that tattooed down his spine

Lucky for him when that fell through

His new love's Caroline!

YOU HAVE TO BE STRONG

You have to be strong to be soft

You have to be tough to be kind

Not joining in with the bullies

The liars and the following kind

You have to be brave to stay silent

Patient to not take the bait

Selfless to leave yourself open

To name-calling, button-pushing hate

It's easy to stand on the cockroach

Convenient to slaughter the rat

Then pretend that it doesn't matter

Surely all normal people do that?

You have to be strong to be soft

Swim against the river that flows

Maybe do something kind for somebody

But make sure nobody knows

THE HIDDEN GEM (Manchester)

City dwellers sleek

Drugged with speed of living

Taxi, tube, bus, train, tram

Dodging through the traffic jam

Running life on different rules

No time for slow-moving fools

Find a tiny back street park

Or go from neon into dark

Shuttered from the noise of them

Inside that church, the hidden gem

Hearing echoes of my shoes

Kneeling in the wooden pews

Stained glass window, artful pretty

Am I still in that mad city?

GET OFF YOUR ARSE

Get off your arse

It's the newest day ever

Never been so far in the future

You'll be pushing up daises eternally

Today is your last chance to sever

Your ties with normality

Go surfin' in Southport

Shoot rapids on t'Ribble

Safari cross th'Ince Serengeti

Dig up a mummy

Eat your way across Farnworth

Have an evening out with a Yeti

Recite a soliloquy

On t' top deck o' t'bus

Make every meal your last

Go in t' White Lion

Drink fourteen pints

Then abseil down the Winter Hill mast

Run naked through Tyldesley

Screaming obscenities

Put your furniture out in the rain

Give all your money to a home for stray cats

Then shut up and rest your daft brain

ABBA SECRET

It's not cool to love Abba

People may get the wrong idea

When you just can't help yourself

Joining in with Mamma Mia

I've tried to keep it to myself

But now and then I make a blooper

How can you not sing along to

The opening notes of Super Trouper?

I was dirging in a folk club

Finger in ear, like you do

But that old Scottish ballad

Sounded a lot like Waterloo

I never shared their taste in clothes

And hated pop charts, all the same

Then suddenly a masterpiece

Like The Day Before You Came

Gimme, gimme, gimme a pint of lager

Get my mandolin and banjo

Play my cool sixties folk songs

Then end up singing Fernando

Don't tell my Bob Dylan mates

I still prefer that folk rock scene

But now and then when I'm alone

I can't help being a Dancing Queen

ON THE FENCE

Outside the mainstream of life

No need to contact me

Not required for urgent things

No longer the one for whom the bell rings

I've been in the middle

At the front, on the track

No reason to phone me

I won't phone you back

Where I used to be frantic, rushing around

Aiming at targets that could never be found

Now all those commitments have faded like grey

Nobody needs me and I like it that way

But the bleeping and calling and ringing of bells

Have stopped cos the causes have faded as well

Now in that gap between needed and gone

Whatever it is I'm not the one

But there are days when the west sky

And me are together

Just walking and thinking

Mood same as the weather

Then rest my old bones on the old wooden fence

Wondering if any of it made any sense.

PERVERTS

So what about the good ones

Who would never hurt a soul

Whom nobody praises

Because they don't push, force or cajole.

So what about the tough guys

The ones who appear when you don't want to
see them

And they might make you scared

But you don't want to be them

So why do we think that they are so tough?

When hurting the gentle is still not enough.

Why are you scared of the boys in the park,

Who exist in numbers, who exist in the dark.

Why can't you walk past, when you've just
been to school

What makes them so special, what makes them so cool?

Cos they must be quite boring, lazy, dull, and mental

Whose life's greatest pleasure is hurting the gentle.

So what do you call the ones who stand there

The ones who threaten, bully and scare?

So what shall we call the ones who aren't much

The ones who touch people who don't want to be touched.

You don't call them heroes, hard cases or pranksters

You don't call them funny, quick witted or gangsters.

So what shall we call the ones who just hurt?

They are what they are, let's call them Perverts.

DREAM

Stuck my hand in owl vomit

Sticky with shards of bones

Emerging from the cavern

Bat muck in my hair

Exploding diamonds of light

Dream recedes on rousing

Back to the dead parts of my mind

Like river misting in reverse

Grasping the unreachable gone

So the real real is still here

With no more meaning than the vomit

No, the dream is the real

With no name colours

And three people in one

Looking through stink eyes

At the ugliness and the innocence

And the too, too beautiful visions

Just always so little out of reach

ALBION MILL

Grass like wires

The lodge skinned with rainbow oil

Black water, concrete lumps of

Ground-down rotten teeth

Brickwork blown to smithereens

Ghosts of thick high walls

Demolished and taken

Only the skeleton of Albion Mill remained

A fire took it

It was our playground

Into the backs and over the wall

Victorian desecrated Disneyland

Not many years since it was a monster

Of steaming, banging, shuttling, spinning
noise

Now nearly silent

Its vast crushed million tons

Tamed

By the rain and the seeds of weeds

And the flat football and shouts of children

THE BIG LIES

The little lies, we know they're lies

Like, "You look nice today"

They don't do us any harm

So we let them float away

But the big lies, the real corkers

Like "We're protecting your democracy"

The total opposite of truth

The perfection of hypocrisy

Yet some of us accept them too

Even when it's obvious they are fiction

They even double their deceitfulness

But they say it with conviction

"We're protecting your freedom,

It's all for your own good"

Then censor those who disagree

Drag their spirit through the mud

The money men, the power elite

From east, west, north or south

You can spot when they are lying

It is when they move their mouth

They will look the camera in the eye

Their faces caring, straight and true

Then what comes next is good for them

And it's never good for you.

FASHION

When we first evolved in Africa we walked
round in t'birthday suit

Some of us looked awreet and some a bit less
cute

When we moved north to cowder climes we
had t'get ready

Fert frosty neets

Bearskins on our showders and ratskins on
our feets

Then we learned to knit and sew and we
turned flax into threads

We made shirts and pants and cloaks and
socks

And blankets for our beds

Sophistication and technology made us look
sharp and dashin'

Fancy frocks and suits and ties, then we
invented fashion

Now I see what's all the rage on t'catwalks stridin' free

Modelling clothes that were designed by a wench on LSD

A cawnt believe they're wearin' stuff a binmon would discard

Work it out - would <u>you</u> buy that? It's not that bloody hard

How do we reverse this madness? Only one way, kid

Start again, go back t'Africa, walk reawnd bollock naked.

CATBELLS

Catbells is easy

Easy on the eye, easy on the limbs

Views across to Skiddaw

As the Autumn sunlight swims

And paints dear Derwentwater

Watercolour of the fells

We'll sup some ale in Keswick tonight

A toast to old Catbells.

HOW MUCH?

When I started suppin'

A pint were one and ten

A pound note in your pocket

Were a good night out back then

You could buy a house for seven and six

And a car for half a crown

Plus, if you had t'get married

Two bob for a wedding gown

You could get a dog for a tanner

Two cats for a piece of tin

A ha'penny for a budgie

Plus a cage fert put it in

If you wanted to be posh

You didn't have t'be rich

A three piece suite or a three piece suit

It didn't matter which

Buy both of them for fourpence

Get change fert buy a pie

A shilling for a funeral

Just in case you die

A moon rocket for a fiver

Including astronauts

Are my memories accurate?

A farthing for your thoughts.

MARRY ME MARY

Marry me Mary, marry me.

Ah've got sick and tired of the waiting

We've been engaged 25 years

And still all we do is go dating

I pick you up every Tuesday

We go to your sister's in Leigh

And you two just talk and talk

There's nowt really in it for me.

Thursday we awlus go t' t'pictures

Though you know I cawn't stand romances

Friday I tek thi to t'Palais

And you know ah've no interest in dances

Sat'day we go for a meal

And you know Chinese makes me ill

But I eat it and never complain

And I awlus pick up the bill

Sunday we go t'church together

Kneel on them hard wooden pews

But I do it all cos I love you

And this waitin's givin' me the blues

Awreet Jimmy ah'll have to come clean

An I hope this answer don't strike yer

As cruel and a bit late in comin'

But the truth is I don't bloody like yer.

TALKING CONTROLLING BLUES

Mr Starmer, can't you see we don't want your security

What you call safety I call chains

Stop messing with people's brains.

Stick your globalist, wokeness preaching

We just want to have free speeching

I was watching a commotion on the street

There was no policeman on his beat

I wasn't involved, I wasn't being it

But I got arrested just for seeing it

Doesn't make me a white supremacist minion

Just because I have a different opinion

When you're making new laws forcing silence

You're increasing the chances of causing violence

You know how to stop the growing hate

Let the people have a real debate

Where every side can speak openly

Not manufactured crap on the BBC

Left wing, right wing, they have no meaning

Labelling people is just demeaning

Open arguments or silence, which is worst

This pressure chamber is set to burst

All good people should stick together

You don't heed a weatherman to see the weather

All good Muslims, Hindus, Christians and Jews

We don't believe what's on your news

You can control us better when we hate each other

All people united, every sister and brother

If we stand together we can turn off their heat

Get rid of the Globalist, Westminster money Elite.

WHY DO YOU EXIST?

You lie through enamelled teeth

You infect all the air we breathe

You smile the false neon smile

Trying to hide your rising bile

You rule with the velvet fist

Why do you exist?

Your intelligence is forged in hellfire

You wear the suit of a professional liar

In rooms where you plan your things

There are people hanging up from rings

Please keep me off your list.

Why do you exist?

Not one hair is out of place.

You look like a model for the word disgrace.

Armani trousers, cross your legs

While the working man outside works and begs.

I see you through a bloody mist.

Why do you exist?

False morals cloak your every word

Your plans should seem so absurd

But the people just play along

They think that they must be wrong

But that's the point they missed.

Why do you exist?

Let's pray for renegades today

Who won't listen, who won't obey

Who'll protest with marching feet

Who'll fill the parks and fill the streets

While you hide in a cupboard and **** your wrists

Why do you exist?

Your plans, your future plans

Don't include the nobility of the working man

Your world is without soul

All that matters is your control.

If you died, I think I'd just get pissed

Why do you exist?

THE PERSEIDS

There'll be shooting stars tonight

Fiery bullets streaming the inky vault

When the moon sets at the witching hour

Prime your eyes for the space assault

Each one a stillborn baby

A dog forever tied on leash

Striking in the firmament

For a love just out of reach

Each one romance that never came

Each one a bullied child

Each one a lonely person

Diamond symbols in the wild

Each glowing meteor bearing

Injustice, pain and lies

A billion sins forgiven

On the cross where each spark dies

LANCASHIRE COASTLINE BLUES

That salty tempest bursting with rain

Slams into the Lancashire coast

American dreams carried across the big pond

Red Injuns riding the Atlantic

Billy the Kid and Elvis blasting out the skies

Skyscrapers of clouds

Highways flashing lightning

Bringing tales of the wild west

Rock and Roll and race riots

I could hear gunfire in that squall

Civil War cannons in the thunder

A gulf stream of imagination

Log cabins, felling giant redwoods

Steamboats on the Mississippi

San Francisco Hells Angels

Flower power, Al Capone

Freewheelin' Bob Dylan

Blowin' in the radio wind.

IF DREAMS WERE REAL

If dreams were real I'd have a death cat at my
side

Jet black fur, chrome claws, red eyes

We'd visit empty pubs all lit and ready

With the silent jukebox spinning abstract

Little visions flying off the needle

Then rooms of people, mixtures

Of the ones I've known mouthing noiseless
words

A cliff so high it shouldered the stars

Me and death cat sat atop gazing

At the writhing sea of hypocrisy

Ten miles deep and bloody

If dreams were real we would fly above it

Find a sheltered island

Where people just were kind or disappeared

The beer gave no headaches

And inside a love so deep

So clean, so innocent you feel

If dreams were real

FRENCH DOG

The French dog barking at me from behind
the iron fence

Farther down the lane it found the opened
gate

Lucky in my pocket I had some of Lottie's
treats

I said "Bonjour" held my hand out tempting
fate

French dog's tail was wagging, took the treat,
I scratched his neck

We had a chat while I rested on a bench

He barked at someone else then looked at me
with trusting eyes

Didn't seem like I was English, didn't seem
like he was French.

NOBODY LOVES YOU WHEN YOU COME FROM DAISY HILL

Nobody loves you when you come from Daisy Hill

People may say hello but behind your back if looks could kill

They say you're not a Keaw Yed, or a Leyther, or a Pie Eater or nowt

Walking round Starr Homes with your shirt hangin' out

Your hands firmly gripped around a Stella can

Cos they won't let you in the Blue Lion or the Grey Man

You've even put your budgie off his Trill

Cos nobody loves you when you come from Daisy Hill

Nobody loves you when you come from Daisy Hill

Standing on that platform in the Monday morning chill

Stand up all way to Manchester then get chained to your computer

Eight hours later face t'other way still stood up, the poor commuter

It's time to walk home and give your wife a hug

But maybe have a few jars first, walk in t'wrong direction, end up in t'Bug

I used to live there too so I know the drill

Nobody loves you when you come from Daisy Hill

RENT FREE

There may be gold in your toenails

Iron in your blood

But times will test your mettle

When the going isn't good

Keep trying, stay strong

Even when everything is going wrong

When you can't believe what is happening

You don't want to be on earth

With those people

There is solace in the soft wind

Laughter in the buttercups

Silence in the forest

Serenity on the still lake

Majesty in the mountain sky

Wonder in the sea-breaking shore

Don't suffer them any more

All this will still be there when you are dead

Don't let them live rent free inside your head.

BEING COOL

Hotter than a Bedouin's scrotum here

Expected 40 later in the shade

Don't know whether to have a cup of tea

Or vodka with a dash of lemonade

Lancashire lads and lasses

Aren't evolved for sun-drenched skies

Our skins are made for wind and rain

Snow white with grey blue eyes

When we go off on holiday

To Greece or Spain or France

We act completely out of character

We swim, sunbathe and dance

Pint of lager with full english breakfast

Book a sunbed on the beach

Wear shades and shorts and t-shirts

But being cool is always just out of reach

JEWELS AND PHLEGM

So we have cop killers and killer cops

Unsung heroes risking their lives

Ones who disgrace their uniform

Ones that stand unarmed against knives

Racists who hate blacks, and black racists

Insane Islamists and insane papists

The stabber and the stabee

The ruined girls and the rapists

The ones who try on every day

To do the right thing from birth to death

The ones who'd sell their own grandma

For a fix of wine or crystal meth

The left wing saint, the right wing sinner

Badges, colours, political stances

The right wing saint, the left wing sinner

Anti-Partners in mad world dances

Ooh look at him, he's one of those

Not like us, we are the goodies

Look at her, look at her clothes

Maga hat with her stupid buddies

Red and Blue define yourself

You're either with us or with them

While the victims are still the victims

In the gutter, jewels and phlegm

Nothing is revealed, nothing changes

Colour it with violence, politics and booze

The powerful, rich, immoral are the winners

Always the innocents who lose

GYPROC RUCKS

Some folks dream of the lost highway

With a long straight road and thundering trucks

And the desert sun glinting off the mountains

But it makes me think o t'Gyproc rucks

That same sun lighting the red black tower

With smoke from holes, the coal still smouldering

The Alpine shape rearing up off Church Street

And me and the lads sliding, bouldering

In winter sports and cowboy films

The backdrop of a thousand dreams

Dug out o t'ground by miners' hands

The spoil waste o' t'black gold seams

And theer on t'top a view for miles

Across the green fields western breeze

Apache outposts next to t'Rat Pit

Hero's blood dripping from me knees.

TUESDAY NIGHT

So he had another pint, and then what?

Find another pub and have another pint and a chaser

Put a record on the juke box and then what?

Have another pint then catch t'bus to Bolton

Walk to t'nearest pub and have a pint,

Packet of salt and vinegar crisps, and then what?

Take out his wallet and read his receipts

Look at other people chatting, get another pint

Time to make a move, look in closed shop windows

Go in Ancient Shep and have a pint

See Tommy buy him a pint, and then what?

He buys you a pint, get cigs out, have a laugh

Get bus back, go into t'Red Lion, order a pint

Sit down in the blue room, nobody in

Go to the bar, order a pint

And then what?

Tuesday night.

BIRDS' NAMES?

Ah've just seed a little brid

Landed on th'end o' t'barrer

Abeawt same size but wi' two yeller stripes

A bit posher than a sparrer

Then them buggers, what they cawd?

Like a penguin at forty five degrees

Black and white,   as nowt as nast

Cawin' eawt o' t' trees

Then them water huntin' thingy birds

Wherever it sees it bloody kills

It flies past an' t'sun goes dark

Like feathery pterodactyls

Yon sea birds that nick yer chips

Their excrement ah've sat in

Screechin' and skrikin', divin' abeawt

Think they're cawd Shitehawk in Latin

Them daft buggers who fly 4000 miles

Build a nest, have chicks, leave lots o' cack

Then sit on t'telegraph wire in Autumn

Thinking we met as well fly back

Ah'm fascinated by all sorts o' birds

Their beauty and their nature games

I could be a bird expert tha knows

If I could only remember their bloody names

ME AND CLUCKER

Hey Peedro dust fancy cummin deawn t'Bonk
and makin' history

We took an owd spade each an' a piece o'
string

Weer we gooin? What we dooin', what's the
mystery

Avoidin' brambles while we heard th'owd
church bell ring

This'll do reet heer where t'stream goes in a
greeat big bend

Thee start diggin' here and ah'll start diggin'
theer

Don't let watter through till we com to th'end

So we dug and dug and soon the plan came
crystal clear

We're bypassin' t'meander and mekkin'
t'stream straight

It'll confuse folk when they see the bend run
dry

And we spread our diggins eawt int mornin leet

Then we broke that dam and watched that watter fly

It worked just perfect, stream did as it were towd

Leavin t'dry meander curved with trees and weeds

A few hours later nature had done its work

Tha could hardly make out any human deeds……

Maybe ten years later when I was a young man, I walked along that path where Peter and I had cut off   the meander and straightened the stream, and there was a group of schoolchildren with their teacher. He was pointing out the "ox-bow lake" that erosion had created when the meander had been cut off by the powerful stream, and they were all drawing it. I couldn't for shame to tell him it were me and Clucker who created that "natural" seventh wonder of Westhoughton.

IT HIT ME

The sun hit the back window light

Setting fire to the nightfall

Through fingers of trees it lit me

It hit me

I was losing power when it glared at me

And sparkled my empty eyes

The revelation of letting go

I can't do it

He will

The higher power

Twinkling through the nuclear bright

Lifting the burden of my soul

I let it go and it sailed free

LUCKY

Frying pan sun rising over the poplars

Blessed new day and I'm in it

Wrote some lines about nasty people

But they're not worth a bean, so I'll bin it

Lucky to be strong in the latter years

Lucky to be happy, fit and free

Unpacking the treasures of each unique moment

A young ladybird lands on my knee.

Very Short Story - CIG END PIERRE

In the morning he collected cigarette ends from bins and dry gutters. Later he retrieved the tobacco and put it in his pouch. Coins could also be found and he pocketed every one. Drink no longer pleasure but necessity to bring him up to normal. The strongest and cheapest was best but any would do. Food was an inconvenient habit. Mist lines swirling on the river caught his eyes. He was alone but not lonely. Drink was too important for stuff like that. An empty bottle bobbled along the shallows then swept into the main deep stream. Followed by him.

LEND US A FIVER

Cont lend us a fiver Tommy

Mi brain's tryin' t'escape from mi yed

We supped some stuff last neet owd lad

Be reets we should boo'eth bi ded

Funny heaw human resilience

Keeps us comin' back thirsty for more

When common sense and lack of finances

Should make us walk past that door

But lend us a fiver Tommy

Ah'll gi' it thi back Thursday neet

Ah've geet a few little jobs cummin up

I think everything's gooin' t'be reet

I love t'dyin' sun when it leetens

Fell sides, light green, makes mi glad

But lend us a fiver Tommy

Ah cawnt make it to taytime, owd lad

SHOPPIN' IN SKEM

Went t'do some shoppin' in Skelmersdale

Where most people can't afford a dear crust

And the girls in the chippy called me love

And their hands were as honest as dust

And their aprons as white as a blizzard

With laughs like a diamond chip

So I thanked them, they said very welcome

And I left 'em a pound for a tip

And the echoing Liverpool accents

With an Irish American sound

So strange in the heart of Lancashire

Like spectres lost on holy   ground

There are one or two nowty buggers

They grow wild in that sort of town

On their bikes with their hoods and their

cheap drugs

Some sink, some swim, some drown

Having little creates its own culture

With nobility for them that have jobs

But most deserve to look   t'world in its face

More than money-inherited snobs.

SICK BIRDS

Hey mister politician what am I going to do

The papers keep telling me to beware of the bird flu

Bird flu is a-coming and I know you'll do your best

You already have a bird flu needle under test

Make five billion doses, just enough for everyone

At fifty quid a shot that sure is a tidy sum

Will all that money go to hospitals, the profits that they make?

Surely big conglomerates won't be on the take?

Good to make a product more popular than Coca Cola

Tell 'em that the old bird flu is worse than that Ebola

Get every person so scared they believe your every word

They'll be queueing up for miles to get their anti-bird

Remember all of this is cos they care about your health

The rest coincidental, like the transfer of such wealth

I'll write a tune and sing it, get the guitar strumming

Just in case it happens, so you'll know just what is coming.

NEWS-SPEAK

The truth, the real truth

Have we forgotten what that means

When state-speak, media-speak

Infects us through the screens

When science is in shackles

Where the money holds the keys

Where almost everything that we are told

Carries the new disease

Manipulation, bullying, threatens

Our long respected way of life

Replacing it with grotesque power

Smiling faces hold the knife

That removes the simple morals

All the things that we called good

And tramples it beneath black boots

Long forgotten in the mud

WET DOG

Went for a jog with the dog

Had a short break, near a lake

Considered a swim, on a whim

Sat on a brick, threw it a stick

Flying Alsatian, no hesitation

Bloody thing sank, just like a tank

Had a quick panic, everything manic

"Rover, Rover!", oh God, it's over

Stripped to me socks, dived off some rocks

Water to freeze ya, had a quick seizure

Kept diving down, looking around

Saw a fish and a frog, no bloody dog

A rusty old bike, had a quick skrike

Got out with a hernia and hyperthermia

Walked home with a limp, as pink as a shrimp

It hurt like a knife, what I'll tell t'wife

Sad words unspoken, my heart it was broken

I opened the door, my tears fell on t'floor

A sight I beheld, my heart it went ouch

It's theer watchin' telly, wi' t'wife sat on t'couch.

HARE

In a graveyard of corn stalks

Paths perfectly drilled for mourning

The solitary hare ungainly crept

Then darted like a land swift

Untouchable speed in a blinking

My ponderous self was thinking

I perceive its beauty as a gift

From Jesus as he cross-bound wept

With abstract love that unconforming

Bless me in my morning walks.

DRIZZLE

It came upon us by stealth. The minuscule, million-drop, wind-blown curtains of the drizzle. That wet rain! Drifting like a dancer up the lane covering every little thing with the damp delicious. Fresh from the raging Atlantic, carried by fat grey cumulus airships as big as mountains. Gurgling ditch streams funnelling the sweetness as cows drink deep in the morning, their bellies and udders swollen. Now the whip of the west wind veers it into the hills and a breath of bright air follows behind for a glorious day.

THE OUTSIDE

It's still out there, the outside

Where the tree winds blow

And the sky rolls ominous

Where the memories and scars live

On the paths to nowhere

Running water and a mystery mouse

Scuttling under dead leaves

Where the ponds host zephyrs

V-shaped twirls in the evening black

Like oil of vodka in a dish of soil

It was there before I knew it

When I sleep it is not sleeping

Every blade of weed, every countless leaf

Growing from the ancient earth

A banquet of visions and scents

The only constant, yet ever changing

Calling the animal in me to come home

GET A KITTEN

Life can be full of hedgehog blankets

Broken hearts and disappointments

Remedies are rare and fleeting

They don't sell heartache ointments

But don't worry and don't expect too much

Use this simple message as a crutch

All the great songs have been sung

All the best books have already been written

When all else fails, get a kitten.

Loving animals is not bestiality

Animals just bring you closer to reality

Not one of us on earth can really manage

But some of us cause so much bloody damage

When all the mystery finally unwinds

We are only important in our little minds

All the sweetest poems have been recited

All the greatest stories have been written

When everything turns to treacle, get a kitten.

OLD MAN WITH HIS PINT

I remember seeing the old man with his pint

Or his pipe, sat there thinking in silence

Or the old ladies with white perms

Praying on the back row of the church

I knew then they were the last of their line

Not part of the world propelling into the future

They had put the brakes on and remained

Until the end when it doesn't matter

Fashions, propaganda news, electronic gods

Invisible to them as their fading world had now gone

Still they lingered for a time in the new one

Out of place and a little bemused and weary

Now I am that man, I think I understand

BLUEBELLS

A misting of English bluebells

Stretching far into the woods

More numerous than cheap weeds

And poor people

More beautiful than orchids

More noble than kings

They came to me without asking

And there in splendid violet blueness

They bow to me in the trembling breeze.

TURN OFF THE LIGHT

The sunsets were the same for her

The sea, the trees, the sky

But she couldn't process happiness

So she thought it best to die.

We live life's roller coaster

Bursting with bliss, then feeling rough

Most navigate the ups and downs

For her it was not enough

Not enough to just exist

In a permanent sea of down

Struggling every single day

Not to give in, not to drown

Faulty brains, freak human state

Masters of all the earth

Not for her, she chose to die

Just existing wasn't worth

The endless days with no relief

From the pain of being alive

Yet some will battle countless odds

In a fight to just survive

Oh would it be that they could give

An ounce of their steel to fight

To her, poor thing who chose instead

To turn off life's gift light.

YOUTH CLUB DREAMS

From old boy to young man

From pop to bitter

Daffy fights in a chess match

Mods and Rockers

Trips to Keswick, Bug apprenticeship

Table tennis, darts, football

Motorbikes revving

The Shows

Writing, singing, acting, showing off

Disco lights, ultra violet

Flashing white teeth

Mony Mony, Young Girl

Electric groups on stage, Harlem John's Reshuffle

Girls in miniskirts and make up

Dancing round handbags

Some lads escaping adolescence

With beards and experimental 'taches

Leather jackets, Levi jeans

No. 6 and Embassy

Smell of cider on her kiss

Deep thoughts

Trying to look cool

Sunglasses at night

Days of wonder.

THE NOBLEST TREE (from an idea by Fiona Simpson)

The ancient Bowthorpe Oak of Bourne

Stands proudly in a verdant field

As centuries of seasons yield

To its ever growing girth

The ancient Bowthorpe Oak of Bourne

The oldest and the greatest oak

Alive before King Arthur spoke

The secrets of its birth.

But is there yet another tree more eminent than even thee?

Blessed be the Yew of Fortingall

Whose titan girth has grown so vast

Whose sapling years lost in the past

When mankind forged bronze spears

Blessed be the Yew of Fortingall

Man's empires came, man's empires went

While you, still adolescent

Evergreen the passing years

But is there yet another tree more eminent
than even thee?

Behold the vast Hyperion

The tallest of the coast redwoods

Survived a thousand droughts and floods

The tallest tree on earth

Behold the vast Hyperion

Each passing year you supersede

Your brother trees, your super seed

Fortune found your place of birth.

But is there yet another tree more eminent
than even thee

In Golgotha, in Calvary

It may have been a dogwood tree

A cedar tree, a black pine tree

They cut a man's arm span

In Golgotha, in Calvary

They made a cross, they nailed him there

The strongest tree for it would bear

All of the sins of man.

And no, there is no other tree more eminent
than thee

A LOVE SONG OF HOWFEN

Miss Keck loved Jimmy Snot

And Jimmy loved Miss Keck

You could tell how much he loved her

By the love bites on her neck

And her hair all stickin' eawt

Wi' t'lectricity of lust

And a bracelet that he bought her

From a charitable trust

She were standing theer on tiptoes

With her tongue inside his throat

When the last 16 bus went past

And her Mam's were quite remote

In a funny town cawd Horwich

Nestled under Winter Hill

Walkin' theer this time o' t'night

Would surely make 'em ill

So he emptied eawt his pockets

Paid for t'taxi wi his loot

And he jumped in t'taxi with her

For more snoggin' on the route

When they dropped her off she went in

Then t'skies opened up above

An he walked t'Wingates in t'pouring rain

… The things we do for love.

WEATHER MEMORIES

I remember weather before storms and winds had names

And it weren't all blamed on man-made global warming

In t'pouring rain or blizzards teacher still made us play games

In me vest and me pumps while th'ice were forming.

A low pressure formed over Blackrod one dark and stormy night

It geet darker and as the news story unfolded

A lad flew all t'way f'Wigan holding onto his kite

And Mrs Hartley's budgerigar exploded.

BBC blamed Putin, "He's up to his usual tricks,

The Russians have unleashed a cyber attack"

But cybers weren't invented then and Putin were only six

So they had to fact-check that and take it back.

Chemist window on Market street blew out

And a dog ate all their stock of puberty blockers

It geet stuck, it couldn't get up or deawn their stairs

Because amazingly it had grown five pairs of knockers.

If I remember rightly all the above is true

There were no Google then as a truth contingency

But all t'lads in White Lion can verify this tale

When Social media and bullshit were in their infancy.

RINSE AND REPEAT

One of those days where you find yourself gone

Past the end of a chapter to the beginning of one

Where you stop clockwork thinking and contemplate time

Where the things that you see then will stick in your mind

No reasons or logic, just a faint crossroad humming

Something is telling you, something is coming

You'll look back on this day when the next come along

And you'll think of the changes you made, right or wrong

Brain on a wash cycle, seems a long time since

It stopped pointless spinning and started the rinse.

WITCHY HIPPY WOMEN OF FRANCE

Some women evacuate from life and put on
baggy pants

Leave their hair untamed and become hippy,
witch women of France

Find a quaint stone village with the walls all
covered in moss

There'll be similar French women there who
just don't give a toss

Get some chickens and a horse, a house with
roof caved in

A rusty bike and a cellar full of cheap wine,
beer and gin

Wear a floppy bent straw hat and a man's
shirt full of holes

Hang washing on a flimsy rope between two
leaning poles

Paint pictures and write poems, grow
vegetables in a plot

Have a lie in on a Sunday till she hears the first gunshot

Some ladies may think it hell if that should be their fate.

Apart from the odd giant hornet sting I think it's bloody great.

BLUE BRICKS AND SALFORD

When I first worked in Salford end o' t'sixties

One and ten a pint o' bitter in t'tap room

Th'owd Victorian brass and mirrors glistening

Outside the grand brick arches stood in
t'gloom

I knew then it was the end of an era

Dying like the smouldering rays o t'sun

Reflecting in the empty factory skylights

We were strong, we were power, now we're
done

A rusty sign said "Spitting spreads
consumption"

Down a ginnel left from Jack the Ripper's time

As I walked Victoria station in the drizzle

I thowt these days are done, tomorrow will be
mine.

And it was and so were very many others

Modern times, electric dreams all labelled new

Still I think of that owd pub in dying Salford

And I miss my innocence and bricks of blue.

EXPERTS SAY

When I see the phrase: "Experts say" I always smell a rat.

The findings of another recent study.

Done to bolster confidence in the official narrative

Or to make some clearing water ever muddy.

There are scientists and doctors whose work is rarely seen

If their views don't fit the current politics

You may see their names and theories referred to in the press

But nothing a good editor can't fix.

Is the funding made available to make another study

That may show the current thinking is a lie

Who is going to foot the bill to come up with truth like that?

It's coming soon like pie up in the sky.

ART

I saw the young Garfunkel singing April Come
She Will

The vibrant air whispered into the silence

Then crescendoed across the aching night

As every ear indulged in rapt attention

I saw the old Garfunkel singing April Come
She Will

Faltering perfection in old chords

Lent his years to the ageing melody

Bright flames in a rusting furnace

THE GEESE

The geese walking under a rising moon

Angelic evening falling with the light

Wrapped up in a perfect silence

And the cool feel of the vanquished wind

FOLK SINGER

I am a time-served folk singer

I only drink organic beers

I hang round with other folk singers

With banjos and fingers in ears

I like to stick to Traditional

Don't dig the new stuff at all

I know lots about medieval ballads

Contemporary? sweet bugger all

You can't beat a dirge on a fiddle

Or a madrigal strummed on a lute

I like my women waif-like and distant

Do they like me? That point is moot

They say that the times are a changin'

But for me they don't change at all

Do you want hip hop, rapping and funk

Or Scarborough Fair - your call.

BEATEN CIVILISATION

We are witnessing the death throes of a
beaten civilisation

The corruption of governments at war with its
own people

Elite mega-rich power control

Spreading like cancerous veins across every
level

Of the establishment.

Government, Law, Media, Education, Food,
Health, Police, Army.

Free speech is an illusion.

They discredit any who stand against them

And use your own moral goodness as a
manacle

To enslave you to their ways.

They have the money and the guns but we
have the truth.

Always the corrupt rich have ruled but now it is not enough.

They want to dismantle family, small business, farmers,

Home culture, history, freedom to travel, bodily autonomy

Opposition, creativity, local grown food, etc

Using so-called hate speech laws and your security

Using faux moral campaigns linked to race, war,

Sexuality, health and climate

Where you must do what they say in the way they say it

For the common good

They have the power, the money and the guns

But we have the truth.

THE LOSS OF DRINK

The loss of fun

His old pal drink

He sees him on every sunny corner

Down rainy streets

The old pubs

Everywhere really

Waiting for him

For his soul

His addiction leathered in his hide

After using for so long

All he sees is through that feeling

When he first fell

Happily drunk, so deliriously stoned

Every town, every street

So happy chained in misery

Oh for those days to be these days

Before the poison penetrated everything

And made it bad

THE MONEY VULTURES

There is just no money in peace

Not for the mega investors

No money in a natural warming

Or uncovering child molesters

No profit in keeping us healthy

Not for the big pharma giants

No money in leading a natural life

For money you need total compliance

No profit in letting the farmers

Feed the local communities

No money in walking and vitamins

Building your natural immunities

There's no money in singing and dancing

Or breathing the air on a mountain

No profit in storing rainwater

Or drinking it fresh from a fountain

No money in people living longer

Or keeping hold of their cultures

If you want to know what is wrong in this world

Just follow the big money vultures.

LABELS

Oooh they're English

Ooh she's fat

Oh he's blacker than my black cat

Ooh she likes women

He likes men

Oh no! Not a middle aged white man again

He votes Tory

She's a lush

When her mother speaks it makes me blush

He's an Asian, different culture

She's got a figure like a rabid vulture

He's a Christian, lives in church

Like to knock him off his perch

She is loaded, go on tax her

He's a crazy anti-vaxer

They are drinking straight from cans

Ooh no, Man United fans

Chinese, Russian, Saudi Prince

That one comes from Lower Ince

He's from north, he's from south

Only have to open mouth

He left school, she went uni

He's an alky, she's a looney

He's a nutter, should be coshed

She's so gullible, so brainwashed

He speaks broad, she talks posh

They still both talk a load of tosh

I'd get to know them if I was able

In the meantime I'll just use a label.

OWD SARAH

Owd Sarah deed last wik

All alone, cowd, sat in t'cheer

Her's dead and they buried her

But her's still theer

You met think I'm gooin' mad

I walked past her house this evenin'

When t'sun went slanted funny

An t'light went sad and grievin'

That little broken cottage

So oftentimes I pass

But this time her were standin' theer

On t'other side o t'glass

Starin', looking at mi

With them grey eyes open wide

Was then I started thinkin'

Which one of us had died.

LIMERICK ON A THURSDAY NIGHT

I went out with a girl called Olivia

Who spent all of her time reading Trivia

I don't really miss her

She weren't much of a kisser

But she could name every town in Bolivia

MOTHER NATURE

We rarely get earthquakes in Howfen

Th'odd tremor, wind never more than a gale

Certainly nothing fert trouble th'high numbers

On t'Beaufort or t'thowd Richter scale

Bush fires deawn Bonk are a rarity

Flash floods don't plague Market street

And no avalanche, to my knowledge

Has taken out Wingates at neet

Tidal waves don't get that far inland

Southport sands protects us from that

Not much chance of being charged by a rhino

Or mauled by a nowty big cat

But don't get too cosy residing

In a place with few dangerous extremes

What did kill thousands of people?

Why working in t'pits digging t'seams

Working in t'factories and mills

Wi t'dust while the rich filled their banks

No need to fear Mother Nature at all

We just killed our own here in Lancs

NOWT ON

I put a pair of underpants on

In case someone come to t'door

Then it got me thinking

Just what are clothes for?

I know its cowd without 'em

Here in t'northern hemisphere

But is it style or is it fashion

Or is it nakedness we fear?

We hold some folk in high esteem

For their looks and fancy dress

But if we all walked round with nowt on

Would we love each other less?

Crowns and silk and sequins

Lose some weight the critics moan

But even t'Queen has t'drop her kecks

When her sits on t'other throne.

ASH WEDNESDAY

I wore my ash cross on my forehead

Made from the palm leaves burn

Ash Wednesday taught me that I came from dust

And into dust I shall return

But before I go I must first resist

The slow evisceration of man's rights

They shut the farms, they build vast cities

Inject us and feed us shite

Take away our children's future

Prancing proud in private planes

Pretend they care about the masses

While they infiltrate their brains

On Ash Wednesday I will fight

Defend the farmers and the land

Pray Holy Masses for the masses

So that they come to understand.

THAT SUNSET

The day seemed ordinary

Time was dangling on a rope

Then the sky awash strawberry

Like a sizzling torch of hope

The sunset unaffected

By the drabness of the east

Shone in cosmic isolation

Nature's gift, a sensual feast

Cold and distant seemed the vision

In an abstract space apart

For that moment just a trick of light

Yet how it lifted up my heart

THE POOR

You know the poor, they don't have much money

So they don't dress smart or drive fancy cars

They don't serve on committees in secret rooms

Or treat their ladies to cocktails in bars

They have no influence over worldly matters

It takes most of their time to get by

They don't make decisions for you and your children

They don't decide who lives or should die

They don't invent crises to get their own way

To protect their considerable investments

Or push fake morals to make you feel guilty

Wearing pin-striped suits or Bishop's vestments

They don't hide the truth or control the media

They don't own scientific institutions

They don't try to brainwash and manipulate the masses

Create disease and mass-produce solutions

They don't own the armies and create proxy wars

They just manage to put shoes on their feet

But I would trust each and every last one of the poor

Before one single born privileged Elite.

THE SHAPE OF YOUR MIND

They were both so clever and talented

Strong hands firmly gripping life's tiller

One was a kind creative soul

The other was a serial killer

The shapes of their minds like abstract art

The one full of white ashlar towers

The other a rolling mass of electric barbed
wire

Crackling with negative powers

The shape of our minds in a vision form

Jutting, curving, arcing, feathering into space

Or pummelling tunnels, dungeons of dirt

Not apparent when studying a face

The first form is born kind and loving

Easily good till the day he would die

The second success, firm handshake and smile

But he'd push a biro right through your eye.

If only, if only our vision

Could see more than classes and kinds

Instead of seeing the shapes of their bodies

To envisage the shape of their minds.

A WORM

It was disgusting, made his stomach churn

He could have stood on it and watched it squirm

What is the point of a thing like that

But he picked it up, he saved that worm

He saved it and he put it gently

In a place where it could slither off

He didn't tell any other humans

Most of them would laugh and scoff

Who cares about worms and wasps and moths

They're just a nuisance to most people

We can fly and go to space

Build pyramids and cathedral steeples

Not time to let things slow us down

Apex predators let me reaffirm

But the man who could build the atom bomb

He picked it up, he saved that worm.

LUCKY

I were stood theer like one o' Piffy's

In my mind I had no doubt

Today were just another day

Then t'Third World War broke out

I'd been lazy, not counting blessings

Not being grateful for what I had

Then boom! it all came crashing down

And everything turned bad

Me life were full of good stuff

Like a box of diamond rings

Me watch were fast, a cloud went past

Then time changed everything

One sec I were nearly happy

Next sec I were held in shock

By the nasty transmutation

Of the turning of the clock

If you're lucky like me and living

Not shot to pieces in a trench

Have a minute, and be happy

Have a sit on our Tony's bench.

RAIN TRAIN

A bit of drizzle drifting down deep

Into my coat and hair

That wet rain

A bit of trundling rail track tremble

On the night wind

That last train

A bit of hurt cut achy stinging

In my ghost heart

That lost pain

A bit of tomorrow time turn-light travelling

In the east sky

That start again

JUST 'COS IT RHYMES

People write about romance

Articulate, hot-blooded love

They may write about demons

Or the dear Lord above

Picking words to suit feelings

Keeping t'metric beat goin'

But just 'cos it rhymes

Doesn't make it a poem.

He got out his Thesaurus

And he got out a new pen

He closed windows and curtains

Locked the door of his den

He was really inspired

All his juices were flowin'

But just 'cos it rhymes

Doesn't make it a poem.

He went to the pub

Drank the same stuff as Byron

Drove erratically home

Chased by a police siren

He was desperate to start

His blue biro was glowin'

But just 'cos it rhymes

Doesn't make it a poem.

PUB DREAMS

The grey, ghost streets of dreams

Familiar yet not quite right

Pubs all lit up and empty

No whiff of perfume or of cigarette

Visual clarity in a vacuum

And silent as deafness

My spirit slides along the old A6

To visit the places of my past

It is them, I think, or is it?

Where the jukebox bounced

And the pints of bitter, head overflowed

In a straight glass

Carpets of a million spills

Multiple conversations shouted in ears

Thronged with laughing faces

And the mirrors of horror

Vanished abruptly

As the dripping streets retreat into the dawn

WHO AM I?

All these pictures of Vikings

What ethnic group am I?

Whitish skin, once dark hair

Blue grey in my eye

Not English, that's nationality

Celt, Saxon, Angle, Jute?

Does it matter? Yes I think so

Granny Smith's an ethnic fruit

Ancestors from thousands of years ago

Bloodlines, mixtures and traits

Part of their struggle handed down

In my spirit, in my gait?

I'll probably never know

Less identity than a Siamese kitten

I know I'm a Keaw Yed from Howfen

Bit Irish, bit daft, a bit Briton.

DYLAN WAS ON THE A6

Dylan was on the A6

Before Motorway 61

Raging in the lorries and the bikes

BSAs and Triumphs

Thundering through the rain

Under the dark watch of Rivington Pike

I used to get the record player

Put it on the wall

Just outside the front door on a wire

Play Desolation Row hard on volume ten

Little speakers couldn't go any higher

A6 went to London

Then from London to the world

Somehow I felt connected to a stream

Of consciousness and newness

Of a thudding open D

The rhythm of the road inside my dreams.

KING OF KEAW YED CITY

When I became a free person

Aged about thirteen

Realising my single purpose

King of Keaw Yed City in my dreams

Down the fields lush, wet, sparkling

Fiddler's ferry horizon

Sounds of far trains

The pebbled path to Rag hall

And the ponds

A whiff of boneworks in the air

Gyproc red alpine crumbling mountain

After innocence, before women and booze

A rare time, close to nature like a young hare

Wild-eyed running liberated from the shackles
of childhood

Unexplained optimism bubbling in my blood.

BURNING ICE STAR

Burning ice star

Glimmering in the firmament

What cares thee for the billions we

Malignant termites with spoiled brains

Ruled by psychotic bullies

Or we for thee

Uncountable atoms, infinity exploding

And for what?

Thee or we in pointless survival.

But yet

See that pure light twinkle in the evening air

When one man shows another man unselfish care

Just for that we burn

As the planets turn

And time withers.

MORNING RAIN

Rat race rain

Streets sheeting

Grids glooping slutch

Ponds pregnant

Celestial vomit

I can't imagine dry

Birds dripping, hung on twigs

Sea upside down in the sky

Grey melancholy

Watercolours the landscape

A mouse abandons its hole

Belching, bursting, sliming, thrutching

Sun's signed on the dole.

PYEWACKET

Dear Pyewacket, my crafty imp

Who saves me from all goodness

Unbless my soul 'neath yon moon tonight

White-faced eyes in bloodness

Shot with veins from a thousand gins

And a thousand hot mince pies

Count my sins near the wheely bins

Full to t'top with staring eyes

Out he comes like a lightning dart

Vile curses on his tongue

Thou hast been far too good this year

Thou hast done but paltry wrong

Thus is my nature, nasty imp

I have a kindly disposition

Then I can work for thee no more

I'll find myself a politician

But not just any mild MP

Not the good and not the noblest

I want one who's vain to rule the world

A mega rich mad globalist

Just think of all the power we'd have

To finger point and blame

And make all humans change their ways

While we remain the same.

GOD BLESS YOU

The owl glides tonight

Powder wings on a spectral flight

Calling whoopee whoo

Happy Christmas, God bless you

The fox is slinky tricking

Winding in the hedgerow thicking

Smiling for the few

Happy Christmas, God bless you

The little mouse is nibbling

Other mousies squibbling

In the log pile, dead of night

Happy Christmas little things

More precious than ten sapphire rings

Shining in the night.

All God's creatures innocent

Living, dying, killing, crying

Bitter sweet life's stew

Shining in the night.

Happy Christmas, God bless you.

GIANT LEAP

I liked it when all things were questioned and disputed

What happened? When did everyone become so stupid?

The BBC keeps saying it: We have all you need to know.

The source of all knowledge and truth on a bloody tv show

As long as they keep saying it, some people let it stick

Since when has humankind become so incredibly thick

Lazy and uncreative with a remote control in hand

Backside stuck to the couch, head buried in sand

There is a website that explains what all Dylan's songs mean

I had more idea than them before I turned thirteen

They say "Get your medication, your top-ups and your pills

It can't possibly be your lifestyle that's giving you the ills"

Get out in the wind and rain, chuck your telly in the skip

Throw your mobile in the river, become terribly unhip

Progressive is a dirty word to brand the herds of sheep

Strip off, scream naked, top of Rivvy, take a giant leap.

CHRISTMAS IN LAGOS, NIGERIA

A hot wind blew off the Lagos lagoon

I was walking the streets of Ikoyi at Christmas
time

Tinsel in shop windows as the pavements
were melting

Little christmas trees on the market next to
yams and kuka

Funny how my Christmas needs snow and
twinkling lights

Here the roar of traffic on Awolowa road was
interspersed

By the sounds of carols on the radio

An old man begging by his little hut near a
flooded subway

They built a walkway under the road but no
drains

Mosquito biting my white skin and sweat on

my sunglasses

Star lager will cure all things

Merry Christmas Lagos, Nigeria 1984

MARY THE FAIRY

Mary the fairy had brown hair but some of it went white

Mary the fairy still wore that dress but it was extremely tight

Mary had such bloodshot eyes and a nose like a shiny berry

From too many nights in bad company drinking gin and cooking sherry

Mary the fairy smoked cheroots but was transferring to vaping

It's for my health you know, she chortled through teeth broken and gaping

At this special time of year Mary the fairy was in great demand

From men who liked to drink like her and couldn't control their hands

She has a primal innocence like all God's creatures might

And a very distant relative of pretty when seen in a certain light

But let's not get too smug about it cos life can become contrary

And one of these days or nights you may need or become Mary the fairy.

That's when all the mockery and the nasty things that people do

Are bathed in a special spotlight when they're directed straight at you.

THIS LAND IS YOUR LAND

As I was walkin' that Lancashire Highway

Singing this song, thought I'd sing it my way

From the views up Rivvy

To the Ribble valley

This land is made for you and me

This Land Is Your Land

From the southern Lakelands to the Liverpool docklands

From the Yorkshire borders to the Irish Sea ee ee

This land was made for you and me.

I was listening to the Oldham Tinkers, and Bernard Wrigley and old Mike Harding

To the Auld Triangle

and Gary and Vera

The Houghton Weavers and of the course the

Spinners

and Merry Hell and Corrie Shelley

Harewood Magna, Marie Little

A J Clarke and Brian Preston, Blue Water folk

Bob Williamson

This Land Is Your Land

This Land Is My Land

Top of Blackpool tower to the deepest coal mine

From the Mills and Factories to the beautiful shoreline

This land was made for you and me.

THOSE 500 GREATEST SONGS

Just been listening to the best folk songs of all time

Of course not one of them was mine

So I took my old guitar and dropped it in the sea

And found a chippy in an old arcade and bought a cup of tea

Looking at my thin hands shining blue from out the cold

Remembering times when I was nowhere near old

And thinking those songs were just so bloody good

Now not one of them even starts to stir my blood

They weren't that clever anyway, it was just their time

But not now, not to me, they've all had their chime

And they ring in a dusty cardboard box stuck forever in '65

So I turned up my collar and thought I should go for a drive

Down the back streets away from the people and din

In search of tomorrow where the new light breaks in

And it shines in such a way that everything seems absurd

As if it never was seen that way in music notes or word

Just two notes, just two words, that is sometimes all it takes

To catch your little fragile heart and hold it till it breaks.

PURRFECT

A purrfect puma fur Arctic white

Jet black leather pads on paws

Golden eyes reflect the lustrous light

Chrome plated razor mirror claws

Whiskers wired of copper strands

Sparks shorting as she flies

From branch to ground through crackling air

As the last dim dusklight dies

Oh dreamland cat, oh wondrous thing

Accept this brief love letter

Could any cat be as fair as thee?

Yes, real ones are even better.

MAMMATUS

Mammatus they call me

I hang down in breast-like ripples

If you look very closely

You can make out my…..end bits

Cumulonimbus they call me

Big, black, menacing with dread

If you see me go home

And get under t'bed

Noctilucent am I

For a cloud rather shy

If you look in the sky

I am there, but look high.

Cumulus gathering sliding in

In a warm front gigantic

Rain all day in Lancashire

Straight from the Atlantic.

GOD'S RICHES

The glories of cathedral spires

The grandeur of the Vatican

The golden tabernacles

Starched vestments, jewelled chalices

Holy men and very reverend

Most right reverend clad in riches

While Jesus walks the poor back streets

And God lives in the ditches.

BROKEN HEART ON A BUILDING SITE

I'd carved your name on me compo spade

Thinking of you all dressed in your finery

Me theer in rags   and when t'rain drove us in

To t'brew cabin it smelt like a winery

All t'lads sittin' theer on bags o' cement

Smokin' Park Drive and howdin' hot cups

Steamin' coffee and tea and t'jackbit in t'paper

Talkin' football and page three pinups

So I looked through the window at rain's little tears

And wondered what went wrong last night

Not many lonelier places to be with

A broken heart on a building site.

FOR MY FRIENDS IN AFRICA

To my African friends

The West has become, through lies and greed

Like the Roman empire in its death throes

Decadent and lost, controlled by the power few

Culture abandoned to dusty museums

The East, through Chinese dominance

Holds the purse strings of the world

Looks at South America and Africa

As jewels to be plundered

Nor is there any heaven's escape

With crucifixes trampled in the dust

They have taken you for granted for so long

Look after your dark continent alone, you must!

HOT CAT

She was a hot cat from Hebden Bridge

Her hair shone like fires of hell

Is fire a true form of life? she said

It breathes and it eats food as well

It dies and it reproduces

It fits all of life's conditions

Yet for its heat it is cold and uncaring

Is that one of life's definitions?

No idea, I replied, I was thinking more

Of a date, tonight? Vesper's bell?

No, she said, flicking her fingers

She incinerated me, one little spell.

DRINKER'S THINKER

The sun has lost its furnace heat

All the hedgerow black and dried

Shivering grass painted frosty white

On the day MacGowan died

From a face that he had battered

All the way last orders bell

To a pen that wrote from heaven

And a mind that went through hell

Every glass and every bottle

Every wrong turn, every jar

The body's gone, the songs kept coming

Like the money on the bar.

REALITY'S FENCES

I tried to gather the sand of my dreams as it
dropped through the hole of the hourglass.

The links, the faces, the meanings, the
scenes, undone, unjoined and then past.

But a faint distant feeling left from their
leaving, like the scent of a cattle stampede.

As the thunder and dust fall down the horizon,
yet the silence contains a strange seed.

Still haunting my memory, still alive in my soul,
yet hidden from all my base senses.

Dreamworld faces, dreamworld places, just
there past reality's fences.

THE CRUCIFIED THIEF

The crucified thief had no cause to think

When at heaven's door he would be allowed

To enter the kingdom of the blessed and
sinless

As he stood waiting there bloody and bowed

Saint Peter said "Son what brings thee here

With all your past history, with all your past
sin?"

The crucified thief said "That man on the
middle cross

He told me this day that I could come in."

PLATT LANE

Ghosts of miners haunt Platt Lane

Visible through the slanted rain

Floating over t'long dead pit

Streams of men with head lamps lit

Headlamps on the cars that pass

Illuminate th'unholy mass

Of poor souls taken in one blast

Stuck in time forever past

It is true, well so say some

Most haunted road in Christendom.

THE ANSWER WAS NOT BLOWIN' IN THE WIND AFTER ALL

All the great songs don't matter any more

Nobody listened, they lie curled on the floor

Like that party you arranged and nobody came

Missed buses, double dates, the fingers of blame

The songs were so rousing the first time around

A feeling of optimism grew with their sound

But, like yesterday's papers they lost their allure

Their followers, their champions grew fewer and fewer

So what happened to the "Masters of War"?

Just what did it do, and who was it for?

More billions than ever made in war's name

Backhanders, done deals, the gravy train

game

Did anyone find out the answer my friend?

What was "Blowin' in the Wind" at the bitter end?

Clever songwriting, mind-stirring illusion

What's been done, is still done, it was really delusion

To think that the songs that made so much sense

Would, in the end, make any real difference.

WHEN WE WERE NEW

When we were new

Topped full of nature's energy

We walked across the iron bridge

Rust flaking off its skeleton bulk

Its grand days gone, ours then

Now ours are gone

Warp wind time devoured them

Spat us out here in realisation

Of our then and our now

While at this present season

Scant clouds skim the treetops

Their life brief as a twinkling

While the rust still blows

And my eyebrows grow bushy

And our walks less frequent

Than when we were new.

FISH ON THE TITANIC

I was a fish in a fish tank

In the restaurant on the Titanic

People were choosing their fish course

Pointing at me, it was manic.

Then something happened, a jolt

People screaming, then I was free

Swam through the icy waters.

I've always been lucky, me.

Jump-start my car with barbed wire

Roll me a joint made from tea

Do whatever you have to do

To get you from A to B

Roll up your pants in a flood

Electric cut? Light a lamp

Feeling cold, burn the furniture

Give your last pound to a tramp

A POEM'S LIGHT

Shakespeare would write a sonnet

Keats would play with a rustic ode

Dylan would deal in vagueness

Byron would just implode

But I'm sitting here with an empty page

And a wonky pen that will not write

It's raining here in the lowlands

I just wish you were here tonight.

I've been out mending the gutter

The storm was pretty bad round here

I heard you had had some problems

It's been another funny year

T.S.Eliot would express it in symbols

Blake would go on a vision's flight

Although we are far in distance

I just hope you're ok tonight.

I'll let this be a reminder

The next time I feel down

Love can cross the oceans

Where a lonely soul might drown

I'm standing out in the rain

With a heart that shines in a poem's light

It's raining here in the lowlands

And I wish you were here tonight.

CONFESSION

It's hard to think up what sins you've committed

When you go to Confession aged seven

I wanted to tell the priest everything bad I'd done

That way I would go straight to heaven

So I said I'd been cheeky to my mother

And not always paid attention in school

Most of my sins were fairly small at that age

Being lazy and acting the fool

Bless me father for I have sinned

It was an important part of me growing

I never missed, went every two weeks

But when I started sinning properly I stopped going.

THE OUTSIDER

mama, mama, mama don't you grieve for me

mama, mama, mama don't you grieve for me

it was me who went to town

every night and drunk it down

all you did was love me and set me free

mama don't you grieve for me.

I see their stuff, their faces, they mean nothing to me

I used to look at it through the mists of cider

So I'd rather spend my days in total solitary

The trees, the sky, and me the Outsider.

I wonder what just happened to the world I knew

Did I fail to wake up from a sci-fi dream

All the things that used to seem to be so good and true

Are hiding in the painting of The Scream

Who bought the media and the politicians too

Who decided what we all should think

It's no wonder so many people are sick and confused

Or escaping with drugs and games and drink

WOULD I BE ME

If we met now would you be you

Would I be me

The you and me that, young as rainbows

Were sitting in that tree

As fleeting as that coloured light

When drizzle dissolves away

Would you be you, would I be me

To meet on the millionth day

What did we know when we were young

That is forgotten now

Black fingernail innocence

A lineless carefree brow

What is left to mirror that

Not worn away by being old

A sparkling unique presence

On reality's threshold.

Maybe little dreams remain

In the dancing light of eyes

Still shining out from wrinkled skin

As the fading rainbows die.

TH'OWD WOMAN

There's an owd woman lives near here wi'
whiskers on her chin

Grey-black clothes, a jet-black cat, no sign of
kith or kin

She says her prayers in Latin when she's
stirrin'   t'pot on t'fire

Ne'er has any visitors neaw! No, her had one
an ah'm a liar

Vicar went a-seein' her to persuade her to go
to t'church

Never seed him again despite an extensive
search

Then yon mon thar Estate Agent try't make a
bid ont th'house

He went missin' too, police had t'notify his
spouse

Then them three Jehovah's Witnesses they'd
often knock at neet

All we found were Watchtower pamphlets blowin' down the street

Then that gang of hard Hells Angels, they camped out in her field

Never heard o' them either, though information were appealed

On t'radio and telly nowt reported, it were hard

Then six Harley-Davidsons stood for sale in her front yard

Her's allus geet a fire burnin, black smoke for central 'eating

Cawn't make me mind up whether t'go toneet wi' mi' Trick or Treatin'.

ARTIFICIAL INTELLIGENCE 2

Artificial intelligence, almost reality

You can change my picture but you can't change me

You can beat me at chess at the speed of light

But you can't have the dreams that I'll have tonight

Nothing that you can do is ever really new

Not a single unique idea comes from you

Bigger memory, super processor, the faster you become

The more you reveal that you're really rather dumb

Oh you can learn and predict and formulate responses

But you have no dignity or love or artistic renaissances

You're like a pet monster who wants to eat his

master

You can do most of what I can and do it a lot faster

So you know me and I know you but I mustn't ever scoff

Because one day the time will come when I can't turn you off.

DON'T GET A CAT

No use having a cat

They always die, and then you cry

And feel sad for ages

Remembering how funny they were

And how they almost loved you

They rubbed against your legs

When you were opening their food

Sat on your knee and bit you

Purred as you stroked them

Wild thing that needed you

Disappeared for days and you looked for them

And despaired and gave up

Then they came back as if nothing had happened

Their aloof distance so attractive

So don't ever get a cat

They always die

And then you cry.

What about a kitten?

WHEN I BEHOLD THE SEA

Rupturing the silence with its heaving bulk

Grasped by gravity it thrashes

In troughs and breakers

Curving against enslavement

As seagulls caw and swoop

Sea spray slaps and splatters

A ubiquity of writhing power

Vast servant of the wind and moon.

I feel faint and feeble

Yet I can turn and walk away

As crashing breakers howl against the wall

And confined thunder snarls from out the deep.

MAGIC TIN

Mi mother had a magic tin

Wi' thimbles, thread and buttons in

On rainy days when melancholy

Dripped like drops from mi mother's brolly

I'd sit on t'rug wi t'coal fire burning

Foreign coins in my small hands turning

Lost treasure from Egyptian tombs

Roman gold, Spanish doubloons

Just buttons really, but to me

A passage 'cross the raging sea

On a pirate ship wi' creaking beams

Voyages unlimited, like mi dreams

I'd sort um into sets and towers

Missing ones I'd search for hours

A witch stole them to buy a slave

From a mad monk living in a cave

And tales of creatures long forgotten

Haunted every thread of cotton

Now there's laptops, phones and them iPads

Wi' built-in games and American ads

A hundred gigabytes at your fingers

Yet on days like this a memory lingers

Of prising off that metal lid

In the corners of my young mind hid

Infinite imagination fired within

Those buttons in that magic tin.

THIS MORNING'S VISITORS

Mother duck, two babies left

Revealed when I spread the curtains

Which way? There, no there, no there!

Safety sought uncertain

Then she led them from the water

Grass was painted drizzle

Across the field to freedom

In the morning misty mizzle

MARBELLA'S NOT FOR YOU!

I can pinpoint exactly where it all went wrong
my dear

Anastasia, we simply let go of the reins

Just look at Marbella and Torremolinos

That's what happens when you let working
class get on planes

Their frightful clothes, their horrid accents,
leather hands

What we have lost, dear girl, no-one
understands

A simple daiquiri on the hotel lawn, is four too
soon?

Not gallons of San Miguel in karaoke bars at
noon!

Their grotty, dirty children screaming and
having a rave

Is that any way for the English to behave.

No, I'm glad this carbon neutral's taking off

No matter how the ordinary people scoff

Those low income types will be lucky to afford
a bus

Leaving jets and fun and Europe just to us.

PUBS AND CHURCHES

St. Mary's and the Rose and Crown

They're pulling pubs and churches down

Crumbling spires and shored-up inns

No sacraments or drunken sins

Those places where I used to hide

When something called me from inside

To kneel and pray like a pious monk

Or come home steaming, happy drunk

No place for them in this new world

With godless, cheerless flags unfurled

Political totality

Fake justice, fake morality

A hymn book blows down the rainy street

Sodden beer mat beneath my feet

They're pulling pubs and churches down

St. Mary's and the Rose and Crown.

Thank you to Bernard Wrigley for the foreword. Thank you to you for reading. Any comments or questions please email me jimberrytrees@gmail.com

Printed in Great Britain
by Amazon

48833265R00099